Volume 58 of the Yale Series of Younger Poets,
edited by Dudley Fitts and published with aid from
the Mary Cady Tew Memorial Fund.

 JACK GILBERT

VIEWS OF JEOPARDY

Foreword by Dudley Fitts

New Haven and London

Yale University Press

Centenary Edition, 2019

Published with assistance from a grant to honor James
Merrill.
Originally published in 1962 by Yale University Press with
aid from the Mary Cady Tew Memorial Fund.

Set in Electra type.
Printed in the United States of America.

"Midnight is Made of Bricks" was first printed
in Encounter, Number 69.

Woodcut portrait of Mr. Gilbert
by Gianna Gelmetti

Library of Congress Control Number: 2019944105
ISBN 978-0-300-24634-6 (paperback : alk. paper)

A catalogue record for this book is available from the British
Library.

This paper meets the requirements of ANSI/NISO Z39.48-
1992 (Permanence of Paper).

10 9 8 7 6 5 4 3 2 1

To Laura Ulewicz

a kind of dragon

A cold little poem, actually a kind of footnote
to the work as a whole, may serve us as a way
into Jack Gilbert's book. The subject, appropri-
ately, is the art of poetry itself, and the problem
is the tormenting one of communication. Orpheus
is the protagonist, a timeless symbol: the leg-
endary earliest singer, he is any serious artist in
an indifferent or hostile society. The scene is Hell,
though Mr. Gilbert specifies it as Greenwich
Village.

> What if Orpheus,
> confident in the hard-
> found mastery,
> should go down into Hell?
> Out of the clean light down?
> And then, surrounded
> by the closing beasts
> and readying his lyre,
> should notice, suddenly,
> they had no ears?

What, indeed? The ingenuous phrasing of the
question is deceptive, for it suspends an ambigu-
ous judgment over poet and audience alike. The
first Orpheus had a reason for singing in Hell,
and his hearers were not deaf. His song worked
and his love was restored, though in his impa-
tience he later betrayed it; but in this 'Greenwich
Village', these dark houses of the dead where
judgment waits upon insentience, it may very
well be that one's self is audience as well as per-
former and theme. Is poetry a solipsistic indul-

gence? Is Orpheus merely to be overheard, if he is to be heard at all, singing to himself, for himself, about himself, alone? Mr. Gilbert does not answer these questions directly, but it seems to me that his poems are constantly engaged with them. The sense of alienation from one's kind, the painful throwing back of the artist upon himself, the compulsive elaboration of the details of a personal myth—these are the preoccupations that color the greater part of his thought and that engender the abrupt hard mode of its expression. And a paradox emerges. Returning again and again to symbols fashioned from private experience, from persons and places and events that are variously significant—vivid or neutral; poignant, awkward, comic, pathetic, tender, brutal, occasionally plain and flat—the poems insist that Orpheus is a public voice most of all in his solitude. The poet is ἔνϑεος, possessed; his speech is driven by a force that he can only modulate and control; and it is the curious philosophical slanting of this utterance that first attracted me to Mr. Gilbert's verse.

Anyone dealing from day to day with masses of new poetry in manuscript knows how often technical competence is marred by the cult of a different and false Orpheus, the Genius of Outpouring. The ritual prescribes only strength of feeling: anything goes, if it is 'felt' and 'true'; one has only to utter it, and there is a poem. This is the Orphic Fallacy, and it is a true solipsism, vicious because it serves nothing but itself. Moreover, if it is an error to assume that either sincerity or violence of emotion constitutes a poem, it is something worse than error to imagine that because a theme is important, or a significant episode recorded 'exactly as it happened', the unshaped statement will of necessity be a work of art. Spontaneity, whether generous or not, is a dangerous accomplice. I doubt if there is such a thing as spontaneous form; but if there is, it must be the effect of an instantaneous operation of self-correction, a control apprehended and imposed at the moment of conception. Some such process, indeed, is suggested by many of Mr. Gilbert's most striking poems. Take, for example, 'Portrait Number Five: Against a New York Summer', where the laconic beat of the lines—'Like Crete.'—combines with the stuffy *luror* of the scene to understate a whole novel of perversity in human relationships. The form rises inevitably from the idea, or it seems to do so, and in development it gradually assumes a shape that was destined from the beginning. Yet the process looks casual, almost negligent, just as a thoughtless reading of the poem will perhaps bring to mind only a queer kind of brutality; and it is because these initial impressions are so stringently and satisfyingly corrected that the episode passes from undigested remembrance into poetry. In the end it makes no difference whether the composition was intuitive or a matter of minute balancing in revision. The 'Portrait' is a form, a reduction to order, an illusion of spontaneity, a game. When that has been established, we may begin to talk about its truth.

Mr. Gilbert's game, at its best, is driving and harsh. The poems that chiefly please me are those that most avoid ornamentation, both aural and visual, and that play with the sterner syntax of the mind. His concessions to unbridled emotion are relatively few, and it is worth noting that they generally weaken his structure when they occur. I do not mean that this work is frigid, or remote. It is anything but that. Rather, it beats with an energy derived from passion contemplated and ordered by a discriminating and always alert intelligence, a mind with a restless distaste for intermission. The poems make few elegant appeals to the ear; they move with a severer lyricism than the poetry of decoration and easy excitements will bear:

Not strangeness, but a leap forward of the same quality.
Accomplishment. The even loyalty. But fresh.
Not the Prodigal Son, nor Faustus. But Penelope.
The thing steady and clear. Then the crescendo.
The real form. The culmination. And the exceeding.
Not the surprise. The amazed understanding. The marriage
Not the month's rapture. Not the exception. The beauty
That is of many days. Steady and clear.
It is the normal excellence, of long accomplishment.

Or again:

In Perugino we have sometimes seen our country.
Incidental, beyond the Madonna, the mild hills
And the valley we have always almost remembered,
The light which explains our secret conviction
Of exile. That light, that valley, those hills,
That country where people finally touch
As we would touch, reaching with hand and body
And mouth, crying, and do not meet.
Those perfect small trees of loneliness,
Dark with my longing against the light.

The calculated abruptness of the first passage is set against the more fluid motion of the second, but the voice is really the same in each. It is a voice trained in its art,

confident in the hard-
found mastery,

entirely aware of the difficulties that it will encounter, speaking steadily and clearly 'The beauty / That is of many days.' Such a voice deserves an audience with ears.

DUDLEY FITTS

CONTENTS

IN DISPRAISE OF POETRY

When the King of Siam disliked a courtier,
He gave him a beautiful white elephant.
The miracle beast deserved such ritual
That to care for him properly meant ruin.
Yet to care for him improperly was worse.
It appears the gift could not be refused.

PERSPECTIVE HE WOULD MUTTER GOING TO BED

for Robert Duncan

"Perspective," he would mutter, going to bed.
"Oh che dolce cosa è questa
Prospettiva." Uccello. Bird.

And I am as greedy of her, that the black
Horse of the literal world might come
Directly on me. Perspective. A place

To stand. To receive. A place to go
Into from. The earth by language.

Who can imagine antelope silent
Under the night rain, the Gulf
At Biloxi at night else? I remember

In Mexico a man and a boy painting
An adobe house magenta and crimson
Who thought they were painting it red. Or pretty.

So neither saw the brown mountains
Move to manage that great house.

The horse wades in the city of grammar.

ELEPHANTS

for Jean McLean

The great foreign trees and turtles burn
As pharos, demanding my house continue ahead.
In my blood all night the statues counsel return.

I walk my mornings in hope of tigers that yearn
For absolute orchards and the grace of rivers, but instead
The great foreign trees and turtles burn

Down my life, driving my hands from the fern
Of tenderness that crippled and stopped the Roman bed
In my blood. All night the statues counsel return

Even so, gesturing toward Cézanne and stern
Styles of voyaging broken and blessed. "It is the dead
The great foreign trees and turtles burn

To momentary brilliance," they say. "Such as earn
Their heat only from the violation they wed."
In my blood all night the statues counsel return

To the measure that passionate Athenian dancers learn.
But though I assent, the worn elephants that bred
The great foreign trees and turtles burn
In my blood all night the statues, counsel, return.

AND SHE WAITING

Always I have been afraid
of this moment:
of the return to love
with perspective.

I see these breasts
with the others.
I touch this mouth
and the others.
I command this heart
as the others.
I know exactly
what to say.

Innocence has gone
out of me.
The song.
The song, suddenly,
has gone out
of me.

IT MAY BE NO ONE
SHOULD BE OPENED

You know I am serious about the whales.
Their moving huge through that darkness,
Silent.
It is intolerable.
Or Crivelli, with his fruit.
The Japanese.
Or the white flesh of casaba melons
Always in darkness.
That darkness unopened from the beginning.
The small emptiness at the middle
In darkness.
As virgins.
The landscape unlighted.
Lighted by me.
Lighted as my hands
In the darkroom
Pinching film on the spindle
In absolute dark.
The work difficult
And my hands soon large and brilliant.
Virgins.
Whales.
Darkness and Lauds.
But it may be that no one should be opened.
The deer come back to the feeding station
At the suddenly open season.
The girls find second loves.
Semele was blasted
Looking on the whale
in even his lesser panoply.
It was the excellent Socrates ruined Athens.

Now you have fallen crazy
And I have run away.
It's not the dreams.
It's this love of you
That grows in me
Malignant.

HOUSE ON THE CALIFORNIA MOUNTAIN

one   All at once these owls
waiting under the white eaves
my burrowing heart

one   In your bright climate
three machines and a tiger
promote my still life

one   All this rainless month
hearing the terrible sound
of apples at night

one   Above the bright bay
a white bird tilting to dark
for only me now

one   You sent loud young men
to collect your well-known things
it may be kindness

one   The pear tree is dead
our garden full of winter
only silence grows

one   A tin bird turning
across the tarnished water
for not even me

one   Always I will live
in that Green Castle with rain
and my ugly love

MYSELF CONSIDERED AS THE
MONSTER IN THE FOREGROUND

This monster inhabits no classical world.
Nor Sienese. He ranges the Village
And the Colosseum of Times Square.
Foraging heavily through Provincetown,
Through the Hub, Denver, and the Vieux Carré,
He comes at last to the last city—
Past the limbo of Berkeley to North Beach
And the nine parts of Market Street.

Having evaded the calm bright castle,
So beautiful, and fatal, on the nearby hill,
The beast goes persistently toward purgatory
As his special journey to salvation. No girl-
Princess will kiss this dragon to Prince.
And as always, the hero with the vacant face
Who charges on the ignorant horse to preserve
The Aristotelian suburb is harmless.

Safe and helpless, the monster must fashion
His own blessing or doom. He goes down,
As it is in the nature of serpents to go down,
But goes down with a difference, down to the mountain
That he must and would eventually ascend.
Yet monster he is, with a taste for decay.
Who feeds by preference on novelty and shock;
On the corrupt and vulgar, the abnormal and sick.

He feeds with pleasure in the electric swamp
Of Fosters with its night tribe of Saint Jude.
Delights in the dirty movies of the arcades
And the Roman crowds of blatant girls
With their fat breasts and smug faces.
The beast rejoices in fires and fanatics,
And the revelations gestured by the drunk
Stunned by the incredible drug store.

Still it is a beast bent on grace.
A monster going down hoping to prove
A monster by emphasis and for a time—
Knowing how many are feeding and crying
They are saintly dragons on their way to God,
Looking for the breakthrough to heaven.
But the monster goes down as required. O pray
For this foolish, maybe chosen beast.

IN PERUGINO WE HAVE SOME-
TIMES SEEN OUR COUNTRY

For Gianna

In Perugino we have sometimes seen our country.
Incidental, beyond the Madonna, the mild hills
And the valley we have always almost remembered,
The light which explains our secret conviction
Of exile. That light, that valley, those hills,
That country where people finally touch
As we would touch, reaching with hand and body
And mouth, crying, and do not meet.
Those perfect small trees of loneliness,
Dark with my longing against the light.

A POEM FOR
THE FIN DE MONDE MAN

I

In the beginning
There were six brown dragons
Whose names were
Salt, Salt, Salt, Salt,
Bafflebar
And Kenneth Rexroth.

II

They were everything and identical and formless.
Being everything, they lived, of necessity,
Inside each other.
Being formless, they were, of necessity,
Dull.
And the world was without savor.

III

Then the fourth dragon,
Whose name was Salt,
Died,
or lost interest
And stopped.
So anxiety came into the world.

IV

Which so troubled the first dragon
That he coiled his body to make space
And filled it with elm trees
And paradichlorobenzine
And moons
And a fish called Humuhumunukunukuapuaa.

11

V

But nothing would stay fresh.
The elm trees bore winter.
The moons kept going down.
The Humuhumunukunukuapuaa kept floating to the top
of the tank.
And he found there was no end to the odor of
Paradichlorobenzine.

VI

So the second and sixth dragons
Decided to help
And to demonstrate the correct way
Of making things.
But everything somehow came out men and
women.
And the world was in real trouble.

VII

In alarm, the dragons quit.
But it was too late.
All over the world men were talking about the elms.
Or calculating about the moon.
Or writing songs about the Humuhumunukunukuapuaa.
And the women sat around repeating over and over
how they absolutely could not stand the smell
of paradichlorobenzine.

If you're a dragon with nothing to do, L O O K O U T .

RAIN

Suddenly this defeat.
This rain.
The blues gone gray
And the browns gone gray
And yellow
A terrible amber.
In the cold streets
Your warm body.
In whatever room
Your warm body.
Among all the people
Your absence.
The people who are always
Not you.

I have been easy with trees
Too long.
Too familiar with mountains.
Joy has been a habit.
Now
Suddenly
This rain.

It was not impatience.
Impatient Orpheus was,
certainly, but no child.
And the provision was clear.
It was not impatience,
but despair. From the beginning,
it had gone badly.
From the beginning.
From the first laughter.
It was Hell. Not a fable
of mechanical pain,
but the important made trivial.
Therefore the permission.
She had lived enough
in the always diversion.
Granted therefore.
It was not impatience,
but to have at least the face,
seen freshly with loss,
forever. A landscape.
It was not impatience;
he turned in despair.
And saw, at a distance, her back.

MALVOLIO IN SAN FRANCISCO

Two days ago they were playing the piano
With a hammer and blowtorch.
Next week they will read poetry
To saxophones.
And always they are building the Chinese Wall
Of laughter.
They laugh so much.
So much more than I do.
And it doesn't wear them out
As it wears me out.
That's why your poetry's no good,
They say.
You should turn yourself upside down
So your ass would stick out,
They say.
And they seem to know.

They are right, of course.
I do feel awkward playing the game.
I do play the clown badly.
I cannot touch easily.
But I mistrust the ways of this city
With its white skies and weak trees.
One finds no impali here.
And the birds are pigeons.
The first rate seems unknown
In this city of easy fame.
The hand's skill is always
From deliberate labor.

They put Phidias in prison
About his work on the Parthenon,
Saying he had stolen gold.

And he probably had.
Those who didn't try to body Athena
They stayed free.

And Orpheus probably invited the rending
By his stubborn alien smell.
Poor Orpheus
Who lost so much by making the difficult journey
When he might have grieved
Easily.
Who tried to go back among the living
With the smell of journey on him.
Poor Orpheus
His stubborn tongue
Blindly singing all the way to Lesbos.

What if I should go yellow-stockinged
And cross-gartered?
Suppose I did smile
Fantastically,
Kissed my hand to novelty,
What then?
Still would they imprison me in their dark house.
They would taunt me as doctors
Concerned for my health
And laugh.
Always that consuming,
Unrelenting laughter.

The musk deer is beguiled down from the great mountain
By flutes
To be fastened in a box
And tortured for the smell of his pain.

Yet somehow
There is somehow

I long for my old bigotry.

16

ORPHEUS IN
GREENWICH VILLAGE

What if Orpheus,
confident in the hard-
found mastery,
should go down into Hell?
Out of the clean light down?
And then, surrounded
by the closing beasts
and readying his lyre,
should notice, suddenly,
they had no ears?

DON GIOVANNI ON HIS WAY
TO HELL

The oxen have voices
the flowers are wounds
you never recover from Tuscany noons

    they cripple with beauty
    and butcher with love
    sing folly, sing flee, sing going down

the moon is corroding
the deer have gone lame
(but you never escape the incurably sane

    uncrippled by beauty
    unbutchered by love)
    sing folly, flee, sing going down

now it rains in your bowels
it rains though you weep
with terrible tameness it rains in your sleep

    and cripples with beauty
    and butchers with love

you never recover
you never escape
and you mustn't endeavor to find the mistake

    that cripples with beauty
    that butchers as love
    sing folly, sing flee, sing going down

sing maidens and towns, Oh maidens and towns
folly, flee, sing going down

DON GIOVANNI ON HIS WAY
TO HELL (II)

for Sue

How could they think women a recreation?
Or the repetition of bodies of steady interest?
Only the ignorant or busy could. That elm
Of flesh must prove a luxury of primes;
Be perilous and dear with rain of an alternate earth.
Which is not to damn the forested China of touching.
I am neither priestly nor tired, and the great knowledge
Of breasts with their loud nipples congregates in me.
The sudden nakedness, the small ribs, the mouth.
Splendid. Splendid. Splendid. Like Rome. Like loins.
A glamour sufficient to our long marvelous dying.
I say sufficient and speak with earned privilege,
For my life has been eaten in that foliate city.
To ambergris. But not for recreation.
I would not have lost so much for recreation.

Nor for love as the sweet pretend: the children's game
Of deliberate ignorance of each to allow the dreaming.
Not for the impersonal belly nor the heart's drunkenness
Have I come this far, stubborn, disastrous way.
But for relish of those archipelagoes of person.
To hold her in hand, closed as any sparrow,
And call and call forever till she turn from bird
To blowing woods. From wood to jungle. Persimmon.
To light. From light to Princess. From Princess to woman
In all her fresh particularity of difference.
Then O, through the underwater time of night,
Indecent and still, to speak to her without habit.
This I have done with my life, and am content.
I wish I could tell you how it is in that dark
Standing in the huge singing and the alien world.

19

Three days I sat
bewildered by love.
Three nights I watched
the gradations of dark.
Of light. Saw
three mornings begin
and was taken each time
unguarded
of the loud bells.
My heart split open
as a melon.
And will not heal.
Gives itself
senselessly
to the old women
carrying milk.
The clumsy men sweeping.
To roofs.
God protect me.

MIDNIGHT IS MADE OF BRICKS

What pleasure hath it, to see in a mangled carcase?

The Confessions of Saint Augustine

I am old of this ravening.
Poisoned of their God-damned flesh.
The ugly man-flesh.
And the fat woman-flesh.
I am tired and sick and old of it.
But the precise addiction is unrelenting.
Even now
It rouses sluggishly in me
And soon the imperious iron bells
Bells
Will begin
And the knowledge of the next one
Will enter me.
The realization of her walking peacefully
Somehow toward our somewhere meeting.
The realization will come
And the need will be on me
And I must begin again.
Seeking along the great river of Fillmore
Or the quiet river of Pacific Heights
With its birds.
Or through the cities of Market Street.
Perhaps this time it will be back
At the beginning
In North Beach.
In Vesuvio's maybe
Where they come like deer.

Or The Place where they come like
Ugly deer
Laughing
And telling me
All intense
How they want to experience
Everything.
Till the shouting begins in my head.
Asking me if I believe in Evil.
And the power climbs in me like Kong.

In the morning
It will be like every morning.
The filthy taste in my mouth
Of old, clotting blood
The vomiting
And the murderous, stupid labor
With the stupid, open body.

THE NIGHT COMES EVERY DAY
TO MY WINDOW

The night comes every day to my window.
The serious night, promising, as always,
age and moderation. And I am frightened
dutifully, as always, until I find
in the bed my three hearts and the cat-
in-my-stomach talking, as always now,
of Gianna. And I am happy through the dark
with my feet singing of how she lies
warm and alone in her dark room
over Umbria where the brief and only
Paradise flowers white by white.
I turn all night with the thought of her mouth
a little open, and hunger to walk
quiet in the Italy of her head, strange
but no tourist on the streets of her childhood.

MEELEE'S AWAY

(after Waley)

Meelee's away in Lima.
No one breeds flowers in my head.
Of course, women do breed flowers in my head
But not like Meelee's—
So fragile, so pale.

THE ABNORMAL IS NOT COURAGE

The Poles rode out from Warsaw against the German
Tanks on horses. Rode knowing, in sunlight, with sabers.
A magnitude of beauty that allows me no peace.
And yet this poem would lessen that day. Question
The bravery. Say it's not courage. Call it a passion.
Would say courage isn't that. Not at its best.
It was impossible, and with form. They rode in sunlight.
Were mangled. But I say courage is not the abnormal.
Not the marvelous act. Not Macbeth with fine speeches.
The worthless can manage in public, or for the moment.
It is too near the whore's heart: the bounty of impulse,
And the failure to sustain even small kindness.
Not the marvelous act, but the evident conclusion of being.
Not strangeness, but a leap forward of the same quality.
Accomplishment. The even loyalty. But fresh.
Not the Prodigal Son, nor Faustus. But Penelope.
The thing steady and clear. Then the crescendo.
The real form. The culmination. And the exceeding.
Not the surprise. The amazed understanding. The marriage,
Not the month's rapture. Not the exception. The beauty
That is of many days. Steady and clear.
It is the normal excellence, of long accomplishment.

LIONS

I carried my house to Tia Juana.
I carried my house through moonlight.
Through dirt streets of cribs
And faces clustered at dark windows.
Past soft voices and foolish calls
I carried my house.
To a bright room
With its nine girls,
The projector whirring,
And steady traffic to the wooden stalls.
Sleepy and sad,
I sat all night with the absurd young
Listening to the true jungle in my house
Where lions ate roses of blood
And sang of Alcibiades.

SUSANNA AND THE ELDERS

It is foolish for Rubens to show her
Simpering. They were clearly guilty
And did her much sorrow. But this poem
Is not concerned with justice.
It concerns itself with fear.
If I could, it would force you to see
Them at the hedge with their feeble eyes,
The bodies, and the stinking mouths.
To see the one with the trembling hands.
The one with the sun visor.
It would show through the leaves
All the loveliness of the world
Compacted. The lavish gleaming.
Her texture. The sheen of water on her
Brightness. The moon in sunlight.
Not only the choir of flesh.
Nor the intimacy of her inner mouth.
A meadow of warmth inhabited.
Personal. And the elders excluded
Forever. Forever in exile.
It would show you their inexact hands
Till you acknowledged how it comes on you.

I think of them pushing to the middle
Of Hell where the pain is strongest.
To see at the top of the chimney,
Far off, the small coin of color.
And, sometimes, leaves.

The four perfectly tangerines were a
clue
as they sat
singing
(three to one)
in that ten-thirty
am room
not unhappily of
death
singing of how they were tangerines
against white
but how
against continuous orange
they were only
fruit.

One sang of God
of his eight thousand green faces
and the immediate glory of his
pavilioned
dancing.

Three sang of how you can't go back.

One sang of the seeds in his heart
of how
inside the tangerine-colored skin
inside his flesh
(which was the color of
tangerines)
were little
seeds
which were

inside
green.

So
I opened the one
and the odor of his breaking
was the sweet breasts
of being no longer
only.

THE FIRST MORNING OF THE WORLD ON LONG ISLAND

for Doris

The provisional and awkward harp
of me
makes nothing of you now.
I labor to constrain it
but am unschooled and cannot.
One learns to play the harp,
said Aristotle, by playing.
But I do not. Such a harp
grows always more dear
and I manage always less truly
well. Each visitor off-hand
does better. While I with this year
of loss can do nothing.
Can say nothing of the smell
of rain in the desert
and the cottonwoods blowing
above us. If it would tell
even so little of Council Bluffs.
But it will not.
I can make it mourn
but not celebrate the River
nor my happiness in having been
of you.

I'LL TRY TO EXPLAIN ABOUT THE FEAR

I'll try to explain about the fear
again
since you think my trouble with the whales
and elephants is a question of size.
I'm on the other inhabited island
of the Tremiti group
looking across evening on the water
and up the enormous cliffs
to San Nicola.
I've been watching the few weak lights
begin
thinking of Alcibiades
and those last years at Trebizond.
I've been looking at San Nicola
huddled behind the great, ruined
fortifications
and thinking how the dark is leaking
out of the broken windows.
How the doors on those stone houses
are banging and banging and banging.
I've been remembering the high grass
in the piazza.
And Rimbaud in the meaningless jungle.
I know the business of the whales
may bring me there.
That trying to understand about the elephants,
about my stunned heart,
may require it.
May choose that for the last years.

A bare white room
overlooking the cathedral.
High up there
with the pure light
and the lust.

POEM FOR LAURA

Now come the bright prophets across my life.
The solemn flesh, the miracles, and the pain.
Across the simple meadows of my heart,
Splendidly you come promising sorrow.
And knowing, I bless your coming with trees of love,
Singing, singing even to the night.

The princely mornings will fail when you go, and night
Will come like animals. Yet I open my cautious life
And sing thanksgiving of yes, oh yes to love,
Even while the tireless crows of pain
And the diligent fever-ticks of sorrow
Are somehow privileged in my flowering heart.

For you fashion such rivers in my soon unable heart
As are focused to paradise by the crippling night.
Such terraced waters as are cheap at only sorrow.
And to have cargoes of hyacinths sail once more my life
I will freely undertake any debt of pain.
I will break these hands for tokens, oh my love.

PORTRAIT NUMBER FIVE:
AGAINST A NEW YORK SUMMER

I'd walk her home after work
buying roses and talking of Bechsteins.
She was full of soul.
Her small room was gorged with heat
and there were no windows.
She'd take off everything
but her pants
and take the pins from her hair
throwing them on the floor
with a great noise.
Like Crete.
We wouldn't make love.
She'd get on the bed
with those nipples
and we'd lie
sweating
and talking of my best friend.
They were in love.
When I got quiet
she'd put on usually Debussy
and
leaning down to the small ribs
bite me.
Hard.

THE BAY BRIDGE FROM
PORTRERO HILL

Pure
Every day there's the bridge
Every day there's the bridge
Every day there's the bridge
Every day there's the bridge
And each night.
It's not easy to live this way.

Once
The bridge was small and stone-white
And called the Pont au Change
Or the Pont Louis Phillippe.
We went home at midnight
To the Ile Saint Louis as deer
Through a rustle of bells.
Six years distant
And the Atlantic
And a continent.
The way I was then
And the way I am now.
A long time.

I fed in the bright parts of the forest,
Stinting to pass among the impali.
But one can acquire a taste for love
As for loneliness
Or ugliness
As for saintliness.
Each a special way of going down.

That was a sweet country
And large.

Ample with esplanades,
Easy with apricots.
A happy country.
But a country for children.

Now
Every day there's the bridge.
Every day there's the exacting,
Literal, foreign country of the heart.
Toads and panders
Ruined horses
Pears
Terrifying honey
Heralds
Heralds

ON GROWING OLD
IN SAN FRANCISCO

Two girls barefoot walking in the rain
Both girls lovely, one of them is sane
Hurting me softly
Hurting me though
Two girls barefoot walking in the snow
Walking in the white snow
Walking in the black
Two girls barefoot never coming back

WITHOUT WATTEAU, WITHOUT BURCKHARDT, OKLAHOMA

In April, holding my house and held
Unprepared in the stomach of death,
I receive the vacant landscape of America.

In April, before the concealment of beauty,
The vacant landscape of America, bright,
Comes through me. Comes through my house like Laura.

Intractable, the states of reality come,
Lordly, in April, Texas, impossibly
To this house furnished with the standard half-

Consummated loves: Vienna under rain,
Summer in the mountains above Como, Provence
The special country of my heart. In April,

Inadvertently, at thirty-three, filled
With walled towns of lemon trees, I am
Unexpectedly alone in West Virginia.

LETTER TO MR. JOHN KEATS

The Spanish Steps—February 23, 1961

What can I do with these people?
They come to the risk so dutifully.
Are delighted by anecdotes that give
Them Poetry. Are grateful to be told
Of diagonals that give them Painting.
Good people. But stubborn when warned
The beast is not domestic.

How can I persuade them
That the dark, soulful Keats
Was five feet one?
Liked fighting and bear-baiting?
I can't explain the red hair.
Nor say how you died so full
Of lust for Fanny Brawne.

I will tell them of Semele.

PORTOLANO
"Asti kasmin-cit pradese nagaram"

In your thin body is an East of wonder.
In your walking are accounts of morning.
Your hands are legends, and your mouth a proof of kilins.
    But the way is long
    And the roads bad.

Beyond the crucial pass of Tauris
Past the special lure of vice
Beyond Persepolis and the ease of Badakshan
Stretches a waste of caution.
    The route is difficult
    And the maps wrong.

If one survives the singing-sands of pride
And the always drumming hill of fear
He finds an impregnable range of moderation.
    Ascent is dangerous
    And the cold maims.

Could one get through, the brilliance of Cambaluc
And the wealth of Shangtu would be there, no doubt;
But what of the Bamboo Pavilion? It is fashioned, they say,
To be easily dismantled and moved.
    The Khan is seventy
    And the Mings strong.

In your thin body is an East of wander.
In your seeking are distrains of mourning.
While Venice is close at hand—to be taken now or lost.
    The season of grace
    May be spent once.

In the pavilion, they say, are birds.

40

IT IS CLEAR WHY THE ANGELS
COME NO MORE

It is clear why the angels come no more.
Standing so large in their beautiful Latin,
How could they accept being refracted
So small in another grammar, or leave
Their perfect singing for this broken speech?
Why should they stumble this alien world?

Always I have envied the angels their grace.
But I left my hope of Byzantine size
And came to this awkwardness, this stupidity.
Came finally to you washing my face
As everyone laughed, and found a forest
Opening as marriage ran in me. All

The leaves in the world turned a little
Singing: The angels are wrong.

THE WHITENESS, THE SOUND, AND ALCIBIADES

So I come on this birthday at last
Here in the house of strangers.
With a broken pair of shoes,
No profession, and a few poems.
After all that promise.
Not by addiction or play; by choices.
By concern for whales and love,
For elephants and Alcibiades.
But to arrive at so little product.
A few corners done,
An arcade up but unfaced,
And everywhere the ambitious
Unfinished monuments to Myshkin
And magnitude. Like persisting
On the arrogant steeple of Beauvais.

I wake in Trastevere
In the house of city-peasants
And lie in the noise dreaming
On the wealth of summer nights
From my childhood when the dark
Was sixty feet deep in luxury
Of elm and maple and sycamore.
I wandered hour by hour
With my gentle, bewildered need,
Following the faint sound
Of women in the moving leaves.

In Latium, years ago,
I sat by the road watching
An ox come through the day.
Stark white in the distance.
Occasionally under a tree.
Colorless in the heavy sun.
Suave in the bright shadows.
Starch-white near in the glare.
Petal-white near in the shade.
Linen, stone-white, and milk.
Ox-white before me, and past
Into the thunder of light.

For ten years I have tried
To understand about the ox.
About the sound. The whales.
Of love. And arrived here
To give thanks for the profit.
I wake to the wanton freshness.
To the arriving and leaving. To the journey.
I wake to the freshness. And do reverence.

THE YALE SERIES OF YOUNGER POETS, which is designed to provide a publishing medium for the first volumes of promising poets, is open to men and women under forty who have not previously had a book of verse published. The Editor of the Series selects the winning volume in the annual contest and writes a preface for it. Manuscripts are received between March 1 and May 1 only; they should be addressed to the Editor, Yale Series of Younger Poets, Yale University Press, New Haven, Connecticut. Rules of the contest will be sent upon request.